Expressions FROM A Pure Heart

EXPRESSIONS FROM A PURE HEART

Published by
Workin' Perkins

ISBN: 1-931130-04-3
Printed in the United States of America
Copyright © 2001 by Workin Perkins

No part of this publication may be reproduced or
transmitted in any form or by any means, electronic or
mechanical, including photocopying, recording or by
any information storage and retrieval system, without
prior permission in writing from the author!

First printing September 2001

CONTENTS

A Word for the Reader   *v*
Foreword   *vi*
Acknowledgments   *vii*

PRAYERS

The Mind of Christ   1
New Life   2
A Reproductive Life   3
Which Skin Am I In?   4
Subjection of the Flesh   6
Crucifixion of the Flesh   7
Self Denial   8
Repent, for the Kingdom of God is At Hand   9
Generation EX   11
A Surrendering Spirit   12
Mirrored Reflection through the Eyes of God   13
A Yielded Vessel of Sacrifice   14
Deliverance in the Battle Cry   15
Acquiring the Initiative of a Self Starter   16
Following God's Directive   18
Transformation through the Word of God   19
Conversion of the Soul   20
Kingdom View   21
A Fresh Encounter   22
The Confession of Poor Stewardship   23
Trust in the Way Maker   24
Unlimited Expectations from a Mighty God   25
The Pursuit of Wisdom   26
Precedence in the Lord's Will   27
Fulfillment in the Focus   28
A Higher Calling   30
Life or Death?   31

Eternal Peace (a tribute to Ma'Lillian Cook)   *32*

Healing in the Stripes of Jesus   *33*

Victory in Faith   *35*

I Am, that I Am   *36*

Prayer for Leadership   *37*

Prayer for Protection   *38*

A Wholesome Life (a dedication to my husband and son)   *40*

The Love of my Father   *41*

A Dedication to my Mother   *42*

A Tribute to my Mother-In-Law   *43*

Conclusion   *44*

A WORD FOR THE READER:

I could not envision a physical illustration when asked by artist Odes Roberts, "what does a pure heart symbolize to you?" Rather, I thought about David, and the outpour of his spirit in Psalms. A pure heart does not imply perfection, but sincerity. God judges us by our hearts. Our relationship with God relies on our ability to be honest with Him and ourselves.

The artistic impression contained on the cover illustrates man's offering of a pure heart unto God, and God's consoling embrace. The writings presented are "Expressions from a Pure Heart."

"Expressions from a Pure Heart," is designed to enhance one's relationship building with God. I pray that the entailed writings will enrich your soul and be of encouragement to you. I thank God for entrusting me to pilot such a delicate commission, and I thank you for your support.

Sincerely,

Keisha Glover

FOREWORD:

It's through a pure heart that the Creator of love pours out His love. Perfect love casts out all fear (1John 4:18). A pure heart is fixed on God and ready to seek God. It is delightful and joyful in God. A pure heart is blessed because it has communion with God and only the pure in heart shall see God (Matt 5:8 KJV). In the reality of being reconciled to his heavenly Father through the intimacy they share, man can easily give "Expressions from a Pure Heart."

Keisha Glover eloquently yet boldly addresses the concerns of life that we all face from day to day. "Expressions from a Pure Heart" demonstrates how important it is for us to communicate with our heavenly Father in every situation. He is not a god that doesn't respond to our fears, desires or insecurities. He's the Great I Am, the sovereign God, and there's nothing too hard for Him. There is no emotion that He does not understand. As you read this novel, you will learn what has been revealed to Keisha: a pure heart does not exemplify a characteristic of perfection, rather humility.

Fasten your seatbelt as Mrs. Glover takes you on a flight of reality through "Expressions from a Pure Heart."

Evangelist Karrie R. Mosely

ACKNOWLEDGEMENTS:

As the will of the Lord began to manifest in my life, He strategically positioned me in the presence of others to teach, encourage and train me in the way that I should go that I would not depart. All praise, honor and glory belong to God.

I honor my husband, Anthony Glover, Sr. and my son, Anthony Glover, Jr. The two of you are very precious gems in my life. Your love and support are invaluable. I love you.

I offer attribute to my loving parents, Robert and Artie Wiggins. The humility, obedience and faith that you expeditiously model before God and others has been instrumental in my relationship with the Lord. I love you.

I convey sentiments of love and gratitude to my "little brother," Kris Rios. I love you and I am here for you, always.

I prize "my PaPa." Ulyssiss Howard. Your support has been inspirational and I love you.

I commemorate my Pastor, Elder Edward T. Cook. Elder Cook, you are a man who passions after the heart of God. You personify integrity, humility, wisdom, knowledge and God-filled love incorporated in one man. May God bountifully bless you and your family.

I treasure Mother Lillian Cook, a woman of unwavering faith. In the midst of her trials, she exempted "self" and focused on the collective body of Christ. The Lord utilized Ma' Cook's obedience to demonstrate what it means to epitomize the unconditional love of God. Ma' Cook remains a critical element in this publication, and I esteem her for the woman of God that she was.

I regard Evangelist Karrie R. Mosley. You are a remarkable woman. The love and compassion you have for people are precious gifts that we should endure to preserve. God used you to plant seeds in my life and nourished them into bloom. I appreciate you from the bottom of my heart.

I cherish Dr. Marjorie Holt. In each encounter I have experienced with you, you have exposed your heart, ministry and yourself to extend a helping hand. Your confidence and good-will encouraged me in accomplishing the Lord's will, and my childhood dream. Many blessings to you.

I adore my friend and "special" photographer, Nicole Moore. Nicole, thank you for your generosity and kind-heartedness. I value you, very much.

Lastly, I honor Mr. Odes Roberts for the artistic design. I am grateful for your liberality. May God liberally bless you.

THE MIND OF CHRIST

Father God,

In the name of Jesus, I present myself before you on this day, a living a sacrifice. A sacrifice agile to your divine will. Lord, in a pursuit to accomplish your mission, I pray that you will execute a mind transplant and reinstate in me, the mind of Christ. Lord, my human mind is so meager; my thought process is limited and confined. In the mind of Christ, I will excel to achieve your will for my life. In the mind of Christ, I will sustain focus. Through the mind of Christ, I will learn to love unconditionally. Love will become the motivator in my response to others. When interfacing challenges, I will embrace them in love through the mind of Christ. I will not allow my emotions to foolishly control me and misrepresent you. Rather, I will succumb to your Lordship, and astutely personify your wisdom.

In Jesus' precious name I pray.
Thank God, Amen.

NEW LIFE

Lord,

I serve you with a surrendered mind, a humble heart and a willing spirit. Lord, revamp me in your righteousness, and steer me in attaining fulfillment in your focus. I declare my will void and acclaim supremacy in your delight. Lord, you are my everything. Absent from you, I am a mere vacated dwelling, but with you I am whole.

Lord, sweep through this house with your Holy Spirit. Filter out all unrighteousness, and purify my thoughts, emotions, actions and reactions through the blood of Jesus. Position me in accordance with your will, and renovate me in your likeness. Deliver me Lord, from self and selfish directives.

Sustain me in the mind of Christ. When self intervenes, I pray your conviction to humble my spirit man, and the renewed declaration to strive in repentance.

In Jesus' precious name I pray.
Thank God, Amen.

A REPRODUCTIVE LIFE

Father God,

I was fashioned in your image a vessel for the attainment of your spiritual sediment and reproduction of life. Chosen by you, I was predestined to bear much fruit, ruling over the earth and the contents therein, (Genesis 1:28). "You are the vine and I am the branch," a receiver of your divine life and delegated dominion, (John 15:5)

Augment my spiritual discernment and insight that I may functionally adhere to faith, discharging the affects of what I naturally see. Fortify me to uphold the standard of God, which is life, and enable life to reciprocate from me.

Intermingle your sovereign existence with my being for the ultimate consummation of unity through your Holy Spirit. Ingest my human inclinations to release the commands and distinctiveness of Christ as my primary nature. Prime me as an expression of your comprehensive life through my daily enactment, for to live is Christ, and Christ abiding in me is life, (Philippians 1:21).

In Jesus' precious name.
Thank God, Amen.

References:

Genesis 1: 28
Philippians 1:21
John 15:5
Elder Edward T. Cook (Sermon)

WHICH SKIN AM I IN?

Lord,

As I gaze into the mirror and reflect on what I see, my inner spirit ponders, do I see myself as you see me? Has deception invaded my thoughts and blind-sighted my vision? Has the plank been removed, or the wool eradicated? Do I foolishly peer beyond my flaws, dismissing your visualization of me? A reproductive cell of the body of Christ is who I endeavor to be. Restore to me your vision, make my current status known. Revamp me in your image, crown me in your wisdom and destroy every stronghold.

The damage is seamless, not visual to the human eye. But through your supernatural vision my wineskins are defected, the seams have burst and leaks stream from both sides. I clearly understand now why old skins are not tailored to sustain new wine. The old skins can not endure the pressure, they rupture and the wine perishes: but when new wine is poured into new wineskins, both are preserved, (Matthew 9:17).

I present my broken vessel to be restructured whole and anew for the preservation of your new wine. Convert my life according to your good pleasure, the Jabez cry. Rest your hand upon me that I may refrain from evil, not inducing any pain, (1Chronicles 4: 9-10). Mold me a warrior for you, Lord Jesus, bless me indeed and enlarge my territory, while boldly proclaiming your Holy name (1 Chronicles 4: 9-10).

To God be the Glory!

References:

1 Chronicles 4: 9-10

Matthew 9:17
Philippians 2:13
Minister David Young (Sermon)

SUBJECTION OF THE FLESH

Lord,

So often, I deter the straight and narrow path of life through the entanglement of egocentric desires and ambitions. My spirit longs to surrender completely to your commands, but the ills of the flesh naturally succumb to sin, and deceitfully uproot opposition to distract me.

Understanding that I am the temple in which your manifest presence dwells, I set my affections on the things above and seek for heaven to descend and abide within me. Illuminate my total being in light of your Holy Spirit, expose my flesh and the sins thereof. The exposure of sin distresses the tactics of Satan, diminishes the power of sin over me and refuels my strength in you. As the spirit transitions me from my comfort zone, I embrace the hands of the comforter.

Refurbish my soul that I may dedicate myself a "living stone," in which you may dwell for the accomplishment of your will. Rekindle, renew, revive and restore my yearning for a new and profound intimacy with you, which converts mere stimulation into continual motivation, for the fulfillment of my destiny in you.

In Jesus' precious name I pray.
Thank God, Amen.

References:

Elder Edward T. Cook (Sermon)

CRUCIFIXION OF THE FLESH

Lord,

I seek your glorification in my life. I seek your disposition and your wisdom. In my pursuit, I realize attitude has a phenomenal role in how I perceive things. My attitude is directly influenced by my thought process, which impacts my perceptions. When others perceive me, I want them to perceive you.

Time and time again, I have allowed myself to feed from the tree of good and evil. Instead of treating others how I desire to be treated, I find myself reciprocating the evils that are done to me.

Lord, it's not about me anymore, but it's all about you. I pronounce the time to feast from the tree of life. When the devil sought to destroy me, you gave me life. When I waddled in hopelessness and despair, you gave me restoration. When I pitied myself, saturated in distress, you uplifted me. When I hunted revenge, you revealed your love. Lord, it's not about me anymore, but it's all about you. It's about the blood you shed on Calvary for the forgiveness of my sins. It's about the stripes you suffered for my iniquities. It's about the last breath you breathed for my eternal life. So I say it again, shouting at the epitome of all I have within, it's not about me anymore Lord, but it's all about you.

To God be the glory, honor and praise.
In Jesus' precious name I pray. Thank God,
Amen.

References:

Elder Edward T. Cook (Sermon)

SELF DENIAL

Lord,

Guide me into your glory as I seek your holiness and righteousness. Remove any barriers that stand in our way. Your will is my heart's desire as nothing else seems to matter anymore. I constructed a plan of discipline in an attempt to arise and learn the more of you; but somewhere along the lines my plan fell through and failed me. I slipped and fell repitiously, until I felt helpless. I could visually see myself lying face down to the ground in hopelessness. But I heard you say, arise my child, "in all of your ways acknowledge me and I will direct your path," (Proverbs 3:6). "Take my yoke upon you and learn from me, for I am gentle and humble in heart and you will find rest for your soul. For my yoke is easy and my burden is light," (Matthew 11:29-30).

Father, I have heard your words and I receive them in my heart. I declare your Lordship and sovereignty. You are holy, righteous, almighty and worthy. You rule above the heavens and in the earth. Your glory is divine and your will, my heart desires. Consume me with your glory. Restore my soul. Grant me a fresh and everlasting anointing. I crucify my flesh and proclaim your divinity. Enhance my characteristics, lifestyle, thought process, attitude and overall demeanor to reflect your replica. Mold me into your likeness. Create in me a mind, spirit and transformed heart, which hungers for your word, thirsts for your righteousness and passions after your character.

*To your name do I give all praise, honor and glory.
In Jesus' precious name I pray. Thank God,
Amen.*

References:

Proverbs 3:6   Matthew 11:29-30

REPENT FOR THE KINGDOM OF GOD IS AT HAND

Father God,

I beseech your presence with praise, honor and thanks. I thank you for breathing the breath of life once again. I thank you for clothing me in my right mind. I thank you for your protection and covering through the precious blood of Jesus Christ. Lord, I thank you for your unconditional love. Lord, I reverence you solely for you, and the holiness that you embody. You are God almighty. You are the supreme ruler, and to you, do I cede my total dependence and faith.

Lord, I ask that you will touch me from the crown of my head to the soles of my feet. Cleanse me of all filth, wickedness, sin, transgression and iniquity. Purge me of all that is unlike you; wash me Lord. Flourish me in the outpour of your spirit; depurate me through the precious blood of Jesus Christ.

Forgive me Father for my foolish thoughts and ways. Forgive me O' God for each and every one of my sins. Lord, in your forgiving, I beacon your strength to turn from my sinful and wicked conduct to impersonate you. When others observe me, I aspire them to distinguish the countenance of my Father.

Help me Father, to scrutinize my sins as you scrutinize them. Empower me to turn to your likeness and reject sin. God, if I can exam sin as you exam sin, and despise sin as you despise sin, I will not turn back. I want to go deeper O' Lord; deeper in your Word, deeper in relationship with you, deeper in my witness, deeper in your love. God, you are a good God, a mighty God and there is none like you; Hallelujah, Hallelujah. Bread from heaven, feed me until my soul over flows. Lord, I see change in me because of the Lamb, and I look for greater change; a change that represents righteousness, a change that represents holiness, a change that represents God. "For greater is He that is in me, than he that is in the world," (1John 4:4).

God, furnish me the compassion and discernment I need to see the hearts of men; that I may respond to their aloneness, and not react to their melancholy. Allot me the holy boldness to stand firm and do what I know to be upright, with forceful impact.

Now Lord, I ask that you will guide me through this day. "Let the words of my mouth and the meditations of my heart be acceptable in thy sight, O' Lord my strength and redeemer," (Psalm 19:14). Douse me in a greater awareness of you in each encounter, that your glory may be renowned.

To God be the glory, honor and praise.
In Jesus' precious name. Thank God,
Amen.

References:

Matthew 3:2
1John 4:4
Psalm 19:14

GENERATION EX

It's judgment time Satan, and the test you failed. I am reclaimed through Jesus Christ, and in Him I will prevail. The time spent with you was the empowering of my testimony. Consider yourself defeated, you were instrumental in ceding to God all of the glory. I am an heir to Christ and a promoter of the newly acclaimed, Generation EX.

Your eviction notice was served when I proclaimed Jesus as my Savior and the resurrected Son of God. He is supreme in my life, He has dominion and He is my God.

The divorce papers from my sins, past and any affiliation with you have been signed and my signature is validated through the blood of Jesus Christ. I command you to get behind me Satan, for Jesus Christ paid the price with His life. The blood shed was pure, and it wiped my slate clean; by the grace and tender mercies of God, my life has been redeemed.

To God the glory.

References:

Elder Edward T. Cook (Sermon)

A SURRENDERING SPIRIT

Lord,

I come unto you abounding in humility. I yield my mind and my total being to you, requesting an outpour of your spirit upon me. Lord, with a surrendering spirit, I request an annihilation of all my uncleanness and purification through the blood of Jesus Christ.

I pray your wisdom and discernment, in haste of a life that is pleasing to you. I seek your complete guidance and control. I have proven to myself repetitiously, I can not enact out of my doings. Victory results in diverting my entire reliance from self to you. So, I give to you my surrendered mind, body and spirit; and I say, have your way. I remove myself from the driver's seat and resume my position as a backseat passenger. To your name do I give all praise, honor and glory.

In Jesus' precious name.
Thank God, Amen.

References:

Proverbs 3:6

MIRRORED REFLECTION THROUGH GOD'S EYES

Dear God,

It seems my world is in an uproar and chaos prevalent all around me. It seems in trying to accomplish good deeds and behaviors, wrong results. I am weary of dealing with self and self-results. Lord, I ask that you step in as I crucify my fleshly mind, thoughts, behaviors and demeanor. Sluice me of all muck and grime. Distill in me your resemblance. Lord, I beacon that you compose the amassed me in your image. My desire is to exclusively replicate you.

Lord, I confess my wrong doings and repent as I turn to you and away from wickedness and selfishness. I confess it is me standing in the need of prayer and change. Lord, it is so frustrating to reach a high point in you and allow regression to set in. Search me Lord and disinfect me of all contaminants at the laver bowl. Make me whole in you, my strength and redeemer. Lord, deliver me from all hindrances and engage in me a pure heart.

In Jesus' precious name.
Thank God, Amen.

A YIELDED VESSEL OF SACRIFICE

Lord,

I uplift you in offering thanksgiving with the distinct intent to come to know you in a most profound way. Lord, my heart passions after your character and likeness. I am humbly grateful for your omnipotent power, and I reverence you, God almighty. I thank you for your grace and mercy. I thank you for your unconditional love, even when I chose not to love myself. I thank you for upholding your vision and will for me, when not even I had hope for myself. I thank you for your wisdom and lessons learned through the varying tests and trials I have failed and surpassed. Lord, I honor you for the gift of life and the recognition of life's delicacies through the affluent love and sacrifice of your son, Jesus Christ.

Lord, I yield my total being to you. I grant you full control of my: physical being, mind, will, emotions and spirit. Lord, deviate my tendencies toward carnality and endow me with a fresh encounter and restoration of my soul. I seek your substance to turn from my sinful nature, and the renewed strength to walk in your holiness.

Now Lord, I stand before you with my hands lifted in capitulation to you. Shine your search light and allow me to see my reflection through your eyes. Allow your righteousness and holiness to take precedence and exploit me. Lord, help me to show myself approved that I may present you to everyone I encounter.

*In Jesus' precious name.
Thank God, Amen.*

DELIVERANCE IN THE BATTLE CRY

Lord,

Your spirit is flourishing over the intimate parts of my life. Lord, I thank you, I praise you, I lift you up and I magnify your name. Lord you are so holy, so worthy, and to you do I give all praise, honor and glory. Lord, I thank you for salvation. I thank you for your love. Lord, I ask that you reveal me to myself. In that, I pronounce self crucified in the flesh and revived through your Holy Spirit with the mighty fire that burns deep within.

Lord, I seek a closer relationship with you. Mature me, O' God. Make me complete in you. Lord, I tire of feeling incomplete and unsatisfied. I desire the more of you. Draw me near to you, holding me close in your bosom, and I'll offer no resistance. I beseech thee O' Lord. Elevate me in your wisdom, understanding of your Word and discernment of your similitude. Commune with and shield me that I may not regress to the ways of old.

To your name Lord, do I give all praise, honor and glory. In Jesus' name. Thank God, Amen.

ACQUIRING THE INITIATIVE OF A SELF-STARTER

*Dear God, "He becometh poor that dealeth with a slack hand,
but the hand of the diligent maketh rich," (Proverbs 10:4).
Slothfulness is of disgrace to you, but he that exerts exuberance
and initiative provides good fruit in his season. For, "wealth
gotten by vanity shall be diminished: but he that gathereth by
labor shall increase," (Proverbs 13:11).*

*Lord, I provoke your divinity and your sovereignty to demolish
my humanity. Purify me of all unrighteousness, and restore in
me a pure heart and a contrite spirit. Instill in me the fused
wise characteristics of ants, conies, locusts and spiders. Though
the ants are small in stature, they are mighty. They implore
initiative and express wisdom in their proactive mission to
prepare for anticipated circumstances. The conies are meager,
but establish their dwellings on the durable surfaces of rocks.
The locusts do not have an appointed head, yet they unite and
effectively function as a team. The spider grips with her hands
and migrates to high places, (Proverbs 30:25-28).*

*Collectively, the animals and insects enlisted represent frailty
with great valor. The frailties represented are symbolic of the
humility in which we embrace you. We must be responsibly
assertive, consistent and wise in the nurturing and development
of our relationship with you on a solid foundation. As we feast
in the Word and commune in prayer, you will unite us in
oneness with your spirit, and as a body we will be uplifted.*

*In Jesus' precious name I pray.
Thank God, Amen.*

References:

Proverbs 10:4
Proverbs 13:11
Proverbs: 30:25-28

FOLLOWING GOD'S DIRECTIVE

Lord,

As I travel on this journey, I pray your apparent direction. In all that I encounter, sanction my persona into your resemblance. Elevate me to your level and overshadow my carnality with your demeanor. Do not allow me to become disillusioned, losing myself in self. Rather assist me in sustaining you as my focal point while touring the straight and narrow path.

This life will present itself a voyage, in pursuit of a divine, righteous and holy relationship with you. My map has been tossed in the sea, for your Lordship is my guide; with you dwelling on the inside, I have appeased all of my needs. I relinquish my weapons, and equip myself in your armor. My head is sheltered with the helmet of salvation. My loins are girded with the belt of truth in Jesus Christ. My chest is shielded with the breastplate of righteousness. In my hands and concealed in my heart, I uphold the sword of the Spirit and the shield of faith. My feet are shod with the preparation of the gospel, and I declare peace in Jesus everywhere I deposit my feet, (Ephesians 6:14-17).

I am a warring soldier of the Lord planted on the battlefield. Through the strength of God and the unity of the body, I will endure until the end.

In Jesus' precious name I pray.
Thank God, Amen.

References:

Ephesians 6:14-17

TRANSITION THROUGH THE WORD

Lord,

I thank you for this day. I thank you for your love and strength. I thank you for your son Jesus who died on the cross, and resurrected that I may have eternal life. Lord, you are so holy. You are a virtuous God, worthy of all praise, honor and glory.

Lord, my heart is filled with pain and sorrow. Pain and sorrow because I have formed a relationship with you and regressed. My heart is not content and my spirit is not satisfied. I want the more of you. Lord, I want to acquire a hunger and thirst for your Word that is only quenched through understanding and endurance. Lord, make me a new creature. Manifest your Word deep within to become a life changing part of me.

*In Jesus' precious name.
Thank God, Amen.*

CONVERSION OF THE SOUL

Lord,

I present myself saturated in humility, confessing my life's errors and deficient decisions. At times, I find myself feeling hopeless. Although I know you are omnipotent and almighty, I often feel undeserving of your blessings. Therefore, I find myself pondering, why would God do anything extraordinary for me? Lord, I know I have not been what I ought. I know I love you, but what have I done to personify the love that abides within? Lord, I need you in my life more now than ever. Without you, I am fruitless and vulnerable. By faith, I indulge in the substance of things hoped for, and anticipate the evidence of things not seen, (Hebrews 11:1).

Lord, implant in me an unadulterated mind, heart and a steadfast spirit. I pray that thy will, will be done. Align my will with your will. Lord, if I am not in coalition with your agenda, I pray that you will remove the requests from my heart and refurbish me in your posture.

In Jesus' precious name.
Thank God, Amen.

References:

Hebrews 11:1

KINGDOM VIEW

Lord,

You inhabit the praises of your people and my earnest aspiration is that you will reside within me. Immerse your spirit upon me that I may become a habitation for your manifest presence to dwell.

Purify my life for the exposure of your radiant beauty and glory. Instruct me according to your purpose that transformation through the Holy Spirit conforms my old patterns and thoughts into "new life revival" for the conservation of unity in your Spirit. Infinitely prosper my expectations to the corporate realm, that my concentration exceeds the personal level and expands toward evangelism for the advancement of your Kingdom. I seek a "divine interruption" to vividly distinguish the significance in your Kingdom view.

Lord, I diligently pray that you will singe every aspect of my individuality that contradicts your will for me. I repent of selfish motives and surrender to you my sacrificial heart of ramshackle and humility. Shower me in your anointing and power that my will coincides with thy will, to fulfill my internal and divine purpose.

In Jesus' precious name I pray.
Thank God, Amen.

References:

Elder Edward T. Cook (Sermon)

A FRESH ENCOUNTER

*You are the Alpha and the Omega, the Beginning and the End.
In all that I say and do, and in that I am, Lord you know.
Lord you know my heart's petition; you know my waking
whim; you know my shortcomings; you know my strengths.
Lord, "I am as an unclean thing, and all my righteousness is as
filthy rags," (Isaiah 64:6).*

*Lord, I pray that you will "cleanse me from all filthiness of the
flesh and spirit, perfecting holiness in the fear of God,"
(2Corinthians 7:1). Fortify me and renew your spirit within
me. Lord, I pray a fresh encounter and a fresh anointing with
you. I confess my sins and seek your forgiveness. I redirect my
soul, (which encompasses my mind, will and emotions), to you
in repentance. Lord, I profess your divinity and Lordship over
my life. Reveal to me your vision, "for your children know
your voice, and to a stranger I will not fall prey," (John 10:4-
5). As you honor the pureness of my heart for the grace of my
lips, I shall inherit the King as my friend, (Proverbs 22:11).
You will deliver me in my innocence by the pureness of your
hands, (Job 22:30).*

*In Jesus precious name.
Thank God, Amen.*

References:

2 Corinthians 7:1
John 10:4-5
Job 22:30
Isaiah 64:6
Proverbs 22:11

THE CONFESSION OF POOR STEWARDSHIP:

Dear God,

I stand before you once again having failed myself. As the scripture states, I can do nothing in or of myself, but "I can do all things through Christ which strengthens me," (Philippians 4:13).

"I proclaim in Jesus' name that the mountain is removed. The mountain of financial adversity is removed. I have given, and it has given unto me; good measures: press down, shaken together and running over. Men will give unto my bosom," (Luke 6:38).

I confess my financial negligence and premature decision-making. I confess my inability to functionally operate out of self. I declare through the guidance and instruction of God, my Father, I will embrace victory; victory over my debt and spendthrift behaviors.

To God be the glory, honor and praise.
In Jesus' precious name. Thank God, Amen.

References:

Luke 6:38
Philippians 4:13

TRUST IN THE WAY-MAKER

Lord,

I endeavor to delight myself in you, knowing that "if you so clothe the pastures of the field, you will make provision for me," (Matthew 6:30). I know worry is a sin and I strive to remain worry-free, but Lord, I have fallen short. Am I saying that I do not trust you? Am I deeming my problems to have more power than the Great I Am?

Father, forgive me for each sin I have committed. I repent and plead your power to convert my darkness into your marvelous light. You are an awesome God. I know what I feel and I know how I want to feel, but Lord, I can't seem to form the words to express myself. I feel so congested and my mind wanders of what the future holds. What lies ahead for me spiritually, financially, inspirationally, domestically? What if?... How will I?... I don't know what I would do... All of these thoughts scatter about my mind in rampage. STOP! But how?... How do I quit worrying?... By trusting in thee. Faith is the measurement of my trust in you.

Lord, I seek your will and your delight. Guide me and I will follow. Teach me and I will endure to inherit your character. Help me to live each day to the fullest as a gift from you. As I strive to become like you, reign in my life with your similarity. To your name, will I give all praise, honor and glory.

In Jesus' precious name.
Thank God, Amen.

References:

Matthew 6:30

UNLIMITED EXPECTATIONS FROM A MIGHTY GOD

Father God,

I come before you with a surrendering spirit. Lord, I beseech your throne affluent in humility. All of the what if's and if I had only's, I cast them asunder, and devout my complete faith in you. Lord, forgive me for restraining you according to my limited capabilities.

Lord, this is a life worth living for, and I clasp the opportunity to experience a supernatural encounter with you. Lord, I thank you for your peace and consolation that massages my broken spirit like the motion of ruffled waves across the calm sea.

In Jesus' precious name.
To God be the glory. Amen.

THE PURSUIT OF WISDOM:

Dear God,

Eyes have not seen, nor ears heard, the coming of your glory. Holy and great art thou. You are a magnificent God, ruling in high places. Your holiness glistens as a twinkling star in the clear night sky. Your righteousness covets as sweet as the taste of honeydew on a honeycomb. Your power and might reign greater than the uppermost Richter scale earthquake. Your love gently comforts my broken and contrite spirit.

Lord, I entreat you embodied in humility. All pride and self-aspirations are denied as I trail your glorification in my life. Devour me in your knowledge and wisdom. For the thoughts and ways of a fool are of abomination to you, but wisdom and righteousness preserves the soul of a good man. I exalt your wisdom for she brings forth honor to me, (Proverbs 4:8).

In Jesus' precious name I pray.
Thank God, Amen.

References:

Proverbs 4:8

PRECEDENCE IN THE LORD'S WILL:

Lord,

My mind runs rampid trying to acquire the right words to say and the proper forum in which to arrange them. The very thought of who you are and all that you represent overwhelms me. In my most complex and intellectual mindset, I still can not conceive all that you are.

Lord, you are wonderful... You are God all by yourself... You are worthy... You are holy... Lord I worship you... Lord, you are the prince of peace... My bright and morning star... Reign Jesus reign... Have your way in my life... My soul cries Hallelujah... I say yes... I yield myself submissive to you... I decree your will... In all of my getting I chase your understanding and knowledge.

Lord, enlighten me in your disposition and equip me in obtaining your ways. My ambition is to live holy and to glorify you. Lord it's about you and how others depict your reflection through my portrayal; it's not about me, or what I can accomplish. Rather, it's about you Lord, and what can be accomplished through me as the Holy Spirit leads. Thank you Lord for the precious Lamb, the Savior of the world and my keeper.

In Jesus' precious name.
Thank God, Amen.

FULFILLMENT
IN THE FOCUS:

The Lord is such a compassionate God, He will manifest Himself to us at a level we can comprehend. He indulges in our quests to mirror his image.

One day, I set out for my work out routine. Upon approaching the treadmill, I programmed the machine with my normal settings, hooked the safety switch to my T-shirt and I was ready to go. The Lord gave me to read the special instructions pertaining to the safety switch, which read, "to restart the treadmill, align the safety switch with the green dot." The spirit of the Lord said, I don't know why you continue to make this more complex than it is.

By this point, I was walking the treadmill at a productive speed when suddenly, the safety switch jerked, and the machine stopped. As the instructions indicated, I aligned the safety switch with the green dot, and I was back in stride again. The Holy Spirit said, if you align your will with God's will, and focus on God rather than self and selfish circumstances, sidetracking is alleviated. Then, the safety switch jerked and the machine stopped abruptly. Again, I followed the instructions and aligned the safety switch with the green dot, and I was back in progress. The Spirit said, see how easy that was.

Now, I'd become comfortable with my speed and maintained my pace without concentrating on my foot rhythm and position on the board of the treadmill. At this point of recognition, the spirit of the Lord said, the more we focus on God, the greater our faith and the less energy we exert on ourselves, yielding more control surrendered to the Lord. When He is control, he has free reign and direction over us.

As I approached the end of my work out, I grew fatigued. The word, "endure, endure, endure" repitiously replayed. As I diverted my concentration from the time left on the monitor and my exhaustion to accomplishing the goals set forth, time and exhaustion disintegrated as an issue. Before I realized it, the machine clicked off and resorted to a "cool down" state. When I positively exerted my energy, I forgot the negative factors. The Holy Spirit reminded me, when you focus on me, and the fulfillment of my will, your circumstances render themselves as a vehicle of elevation. Before you grasp what has taken place, I will have brought you out and have you relaxing in "cool down."

To God be the glory.

A HIGHER CALLING:

All of us interface aloneness to some extent, no matter how content we may present ourselves to be. But it is when we begin to see that aloneness through the eyes of God and permit him to minister to us, do we find the resolution. The devil toys with us when we waddle in pity and despair. But, God arises when we do as you have done, and somehow work our way to the front of our circumstances.

I can vividly see your struggle. I have compassion for your feelings of emptiness and frustration in not knowing why you feel captive to bondage in releasing your total praise to the Lord. I can relate to the happiness felt when you can leap for joy during a high praise service, and the pain felt when returning home to realize the joy you leapt for was never caught and those feelings captured symbolized the temporary condition of happiness.

Know that God hears you and He cares. He is a gentleman and He is there with open arms yearning to embrace you.

To God be the glory.

LIFE OR DEATH?

With every fiber of my being I struggled to hold on. Though the pains grew tougher and the suffering drew longer, though faith I held my own.

I am a warring soldier of the Lord, and we never surrender in fight; until that glorious day the light of the Lord shown upon my face with peace abiding deep within. I threw up my hands in surrender and yielded myself to him. Instantaneously, my burdens were cast, for I was finally at rest, as joy encapsulated my soul.

This battle you fight while here on earth is not one against flesh and blood. It is a spiritual war against principalities, and doesn't require the drawing of swords, (Ephesians 6:12). I can assure you through personal testament, God can do anything but fail and he triumphs over defeat. God upholds unity, love and truth, while Satan seeks to destroy, divide, conquer and deceive.

I urge you to put on God's armor and allow Him to reign as Lord of your life. "Just confess with your mouth the Lord Jesus, and believe in your heart God raised Him from the dead, and you too shall be saved," (Romans 10:9-10).

I've found my resting-place, now the choice is yours to make.

To God be the glory.

References:

Ephesians 6:12
Romans 10:9-10

ETERNAL PEACE
(A TRIBUTE TO MA' LILLIAN COOK):

My ship is now docked as my purpose has been fulfilled. New life is commanded, and "New Life" will prevail. My soul exclaims, reign Jesus reign. Rejoice with me my children. God delivered me from excruciating pain.

No more trials, no more pains, no more agonistic reigns. I'm free my children. I've been healed you see. I'm with my creator, and he cares deeply for me.

Redemption has come, and my work is now complete. In peace I go, so don't you weep. Joy suffuses my soul, for this is a time of jubilee. Presented is the opportunity to walk in your remembrances of me. A pure and compassionate heart; a warm soothing smile; a lifestyle of holiness immersed in unwavering faith. Any segment of me, comprised within your heart, don't compromise it, enact it; be fruitful and cultivate it.

Continue striving in the mind and heart of Christ because that's where I'll be. Your guardian angel, a haven of protection is who I'll be. Until we meet again, persevere in your recollections of me. Representing the model of Christ reinforces your image of me.

To God be the glory.

HEALING IN THE STRIPES OF JESUS:

Do not get discouraged in your current condition, because it is merely a process. A process that will fulfill its completion in phases where each phase presents a new realm of trials. In their most common context, trials denote tests. Typically, we cringe at the very thought of tests as they require preparation and result in either a pass or fail status. In preparing for a test, the challenge presented is indecisiveness in knowing what to prepare for and the selection of an effective study technique.

On the contrary, trials encompass the test, technique and end result as long as we maintain the faith. We can associate trials with tools. God uses these trials (tools) to design us. Specifically in your case, He is using the trial of sickness to heal and elevate you to a higher level in Him. He is broadening and refining your witness. Meditate on the power and compassion the Lord is equipping you with. As you go through this, thank the Lord for the completion of each phase as it fulfills itself. Remember, it is all a part of the process.

Power is a critical element in war. In conjunction to power, the Lord equips us with the weapons of prayer and the Word. The consolidation of these fundamentals utilized at full capacity marks the success of a warring soldier. Now to that, add your wisdom combined with your life's testimony. The Lord is enhancing one great soldier for the battlefield.

Therefore, do not consider things as they are. Consider them from God's perspective. The Lord does not perform any incomplete works. Focus on each phase as a step closer to God's finished process of refinement and enhancement in your life.

To God be the glory.

VICTORY IN FAITH:

Lord

I come to you on behalf of my fellow brother/sister. Lord you know what he/she is experiencing physically and emotionally. Lord, I ask that you cover his/her mind and shield him/her in peace. Peace in knowing who you are, and that you have infinite power.

Lord, embrace him/her with your tender, loving arms. Comfort him/her Lord, and let him/her come to understand the essence of your Word for his/her(self). Lord, let this be the beginning of a life-changing encounter with you. Allow him/her to come to know you as the Great I Am; the Rock that is able. For he/she has the victory and Satan is defeated. No weapon formed against him/her shall prosper, (Isaiah 54:17).

Lord, we ask that you remove any and all physical ailments the doctors have prescribed or projected. Lord, we ask not only for a physical healing, but a DIVINE healing. Lord heal him/her emotionally, physically and spiritually. Let his/her light shine so that his/her life's testimony may be a blessing to others. Stir up an awareness that provokes others to an acceptance of you as their personal savior.

Lord, we know this is only a test and we thank you. When all else fails, you await us with widespread arms, standing strong and prodigious.

In Jesus' precious name.
Thank God, Amen.

References:

Isaiah 54:17

I AM THAT I AM:

God,

*You are everything to me. You are my shield and my maker.
You are my Father and my protector. You comfort me in the
cradle of your arms. You drape me in the serenity of your
peace. Peace in knowing that you are my everything.*

*So, I don't have to worry and I don't have to fret. I simply cast
my cares upon you for you know what suits me best. I yield
my total being to you as my soul cries, reign Jesus reign. In my
life be glorified; relive me of self-inflicted pain. Usher me in
executing wisdom to uphold a mind steadfast in the
quintessence of Christ. Representing the model of my maker is
a lifetime endeavor.*

To God be the glory.

PRAYER FOR LEADERSHIP:

God,

I implore your holiness and direction in leadership for every institution ordained by you. Touch the minds and hearts of the leaders unifying them on one accord in harmony with your divine will. Lord, send them out with joy, that they may proceed with peace: "The mountains and the hills shall break forth before you into singing, and all the trees of the field shall clap their hands. Instead of the thorn shall come up the fir tree and instead of the brier shall come up the myrtle tree: and it shall be to the Lord for a name, for an everlasting sight that shall not be cut off," (Isaiah 55:12-13).

Lord, continue to speak to them, reaffirming yourself through your Word. Permeate every area of doubt with faith. Saturate every area of chaos with your peace. Inundate every area of discord with your devout union. Lord, we count it done. For you expose yourself to man by means of your Word, "so shall your word be that goes forth out of your mouth: it shall not return void, but it shall prosper in the thing whereto you sent it," (Isaiah 55:11).

In Jesus' precious name.
Thank God, Amen.

References:

Isaiah 55:11-13

PRAYER FOR PROTECTION:

Lord,

I seek you esteeming your protection. Lord, cover every limb of your collective body in the precious blood of Jesus Christ. The blood of Jesus strengthens, purifies, delivers, heals and sets the captive free. Lord, liberate us in the blood.

Lord, I pray that you will build a hedge of protection around us. Safeguard and keep us from hurt, harm and danger foreseen and unseen. Magnify our awareness and intensify our sense of discernment that we may adhere to your voice, and not fall prey to the snare of the evil one. Overshadow us in your resemblance and illuminate us in your glory. (John 10:4-5).

Impart in us your wisdom. We cast out every foolish: thought, mannerism response, and reply. We replenish our spirits with the fear of God and the astuteness of the Holy in understanding. (Proverbs 9:10).

We ask that you look on our families. Lord, fulfill our individual and communal needs in alliance with your appointed purpose. In each encounter, prevail that your glory may shine forth and your sovereignty renowned. We present ourselves beaming in humility, as living sacrifices pursuing your habitation. Groom us that we may present you with great honor.

In Jesus' precious name.
Thank God, Amen.

References:

John 10:4-5
Proverbs: 9:10

A WHOLESOME LIFE:
(A DEDICATION TO MY HUSBAND AND SON)

*I know I am not perfect and perfectionism is not my
inspiration. My thrive is for holiness and righteousness. God is
revealing to me myself as He views me. I presume I took God
for granted and transgressed to a state of complacency. My
desire is to go deeper, and not turn back. In that, I have
sought the Lord on what is required of me to excel in being the
best wife and mother I can be. I have never been a wife or
mother before, and I consistently learn new things with each
moment that we share. I pray that God will steer us as
stewards over our child, that we may bestow the necessities to
ensure a wholesome life and lifestyle. Aside from my
relationship with God, there is nothing more important to me
than my family. I love you.*

To God be the Glory.

THE LOVE OF MY FATHER:

Dad,

I seize this moment to exemplify the joy embedded deep inside my heart in honoring you. You have been very influential in my spiritual advancement.

When God gifted you into my life, He gifted me with abundant love. Dad, over the years, we have experienced our differences, but your love has never changed. Even when we disagree, your love surpasses our disagreements and transfuses our terms of disagreement into understanding. The Lord has blessed us with a phenomenal relationship that reinforces the unconditional love He extends to all of us. I am modestly grateful to Him for disclosing you to me. I love you dad.

To God be the glory, honor and praise.

A DEDICATION TO MY MOTHER:

Mommy,

I remember as a little girl, being so very fond of you. I marveled at your determination, drive to excel and diverse knowledge. You did not waddle in the pity of your circumstances; rather you rendered them as a motivator of escalation. As I migrated from childhood into womanhood, I began to understand the "why" in the sacrifices and complex decisions you endured.

Mommy, know that all of your hard work and tedious efforts are not undervalued. The woman that you embody is what molds and shapes me into the woman I have become. I am grateful to God for gracing me with such a phenomenal mother. You are my "Sunbeam" and I love you whole-heartedly.

To God be the glory.

A TRIBUTE TO MY MOTHER-IN-LAW

(LINDA J. GLOVER)

Linda,

I could have selected a million and one cards, but none of which could have expressed my heart so true. No card could say I love and appreciate you, with such compelling inspiration as the words that occupy my heart.

You are precious to me and symbolic of a gemstone. A gemstone is symbolic of beauty and prestige. A gemstone is handled with delicacy and treated with special care. A gemstone is more precious than standard jewels simply because of the value it epitomizes.

I could not have selected a finer choice. You are my friend, my confidant and my mother. I love you Linda.

To God be the glory.

CONCLUSION

I thank you for your time and interest in the inspirations the Lord has aspired within me. I pray that you have been encouraged to progress in your relationship with the Lord; to love Him with all of your heart, mind and soul. I pray that God's love will pierce the hearts of men, and radiate throughout. May God richly bless you.

Blessings Always,

Keisha Glover.